Sizzling Simplicity

A Grilled Onion Soup Adventure

SIZZLING SIMPLICITY

First edition. January 18, 2024.

ISBN: 979-8224728831

Written by Jose Maria.

Table of Contents

Jose Maria

❖ Introduction:

Welcome and Overview

Welcome to the world of "Sizzling Simplicity: A Grilled Onion Soup Adventure"! This culinary journey promises not just a meal but an experience. Grilled onion soup, a classic with a twist, awaits you. This cookbook is your gateway to mastering the art of creating rich, flavorful soups that tantalize your taste buds and warm your soul.

The Charm of Grilled Onion Soup

Grilled onion soup, a timeless favorite, seamlessly blends the savory goodness of caramelized onions with the smoky essence from the grill. The result? A symphony of flavors that dance on your palate. The allure lies not just in its simplicity but in the depth it adds to a seemingly straightforward dish. Join us on this exploration of grilled onion soup, where each spoonful is a celebration of culinary elegance.

Essential Tools and Ingredients

Before you embark on your grilled onion soup adventure, let's gather the tools and ingredients that will elevate your cooking experience:

Tools:

Heavy-Duty Grill: A reliable grill for imparting that essential smokiness to your onions.

Quality Chef's Knife: Precise slicing of onions is key to achieving that perfect caramelization.

Large Stockpot: Ideal for simmering broths to perfection.

Soup Bowls: Elevate your dining experience with the right vessels to showcase your creations.

Cheese Grater: Essential for achieving the perfect melt on your cheese toppings.

Ingredients:

Onions: Varieties such as yellow, sweet, or red add distinct flavors to your soup.

Cheese: Gruyère, Swiss, or your favorite melting cheese for that gooey topping.

Broth: Beef, chicken, or vegetable—choose based on your preference.

Herbs: Thyme, bay leaves, and other herbs for an aromatic infusion.

Bread: Baguettes or rustic bread for the quintessential soup accompaniment.

As you gather these essentials, prepare to embark on a culinary journey that marries simplicity with sizzling flavors.

Chapter 1: The Basics of Grilled Onion Soup

Understanding Onion Varieties

Before you dive into the world of grilled onion soup, it's essential to understand the nuances of onion varieties. Each type brings its unique flavor profile to the table, influencing the overall taste of your soup.

Common Onion Varieties:

Yellow Onions: Robust and versatile, providing a well-balanced flavor when caramelized.

Sweet Onions: Mild and tender, offering a subtle sweetness to the soup.

Red Onions: Bring a touch of vibrant color and a slightly milder flavor compared to yellow onions.

Tip: Experiment with a mix of onion varieties to create a depth of flavor in your grilled onion soup.

Choosing the Right Cheese

Selecting the right cheese is a crucial step in achieving the perfect balance for your grilled onion soup. The ideal cheese should complement the richness of the caramelized onions and add a creamy texture.

Recommended Cheeses:

Gruyère: A classic choice with its nutty flavor and excellent melting qualities.

Swiss: Delivers a mild, nutty taste and smooth melt, enhancing the soup's creaminess.

Fontina: Adds a rich, buttery flavor, elevating the overall indulgence of the dish.

Tip: Combine cheeses for a unique flavor profile, such as mixing Gruyère with a touch of Parmesan for added complexity.

Broths and Bases for Depth of Flavor

Creating a flavorful base is the foundation of any exceptional soup. The choice of broth and additional bases contributes significantly to the overall taste of your grilled onion soup.

Broths and Bases:

Beef Broth: Provides a hearty, robust flavor that pairs well with the sweetness of caramelized onions.

Vegetable Broth: Ideal for a lighter option, allowing the onion's natural sweetness to shine.

Chicken Broth: Strikes a balance between richness and lightness, offering a versatile base.

Tip: Consider combining different broths or adding a splash of wine for added complexity.

Perfecting the Grilled Element

The grilled element is what sets this soup apart, infusing it with a smoky essence. Perfecting this step ensures that every spoonful captivates your senses.

Grilling Tips:

Caramelization: Grill onions until they achieve a golden brown color, unlocking their natural sweetness.

Wood Chips or Charcoal: Use wood chips or charcoal for an authentic smoky flavor.

Grill Marks: Aim for distinct grill marks on the onions for visual appeal and enhanced taste.

Tip: Experiment with different grilling techniques to find the perfect balance between smokiness and sweetness.

Armed with an understanding of onion varieties, cheese selection, broth choices, and grilling techniques, you're now ready to delve into the art of grilled onion soup. The basics set the stage for a culinary adventure that promises layers of flavor and sizzling simplicity.

Chapter 2: Classic Grilled Onion Soup Recipes

Traditional French Onion Soup

Ingredients:

- 4 large yellow onions, thinly sliced
- 3 tbsp unsalted butter
- 2 tbsp olive oil
- 1 tsp sugar
- 6 cups beef broth
- 1 cup dry white wine
- 2 bay leaves
- Salt and pepper to taste
- Baguette slices
- Gruyère cheese, grated

Instructions:

1. In a large pot, melt butter and olive oil over medium heat. Add sliced onions and cook until golden brown and caramelized.
2. Sprinkle sugar over the onions to aid caramelization.
3. Pour in white wine to deglaze the pot, scraping up any browned bits from the bottom.
4. Add beef broth, bay leaves, salt, and pepper. Simmer for 20-25 minutes to meld flavors.
5. Meanwhile, preheat the grill. Grill baguette slices until lightly toasted.
6. Ladle soup into oven-safe bowls, top with a grilled baguette slice, and generously sprinkle Gruyère cheese.
7. Place bowls under the broiler until cheese is melted and bubbly.
8. Serve hot and enjoy the classic flavors of French Onion Soup.

Rustic Onion and Thyme Soup
Ingredients:

- 5 medium sweet onions, sliced
- 4 cloves garlic, minced
- 3 tbsp olive oil
- 1 tsp dried thyme
- 8 cups vegetable broth
- Salt and pepper to taste
- Baguette slices
- Swiss cheese, grated

Instructions:

1. In a large pot, heat olive oil over medium heat. Add sliced onions, garlic, and thyme. Cook until onions are soft and lightly browned.
2. Pour in vegetable broth, season with salt and pepper, and simmer for 15-20 minutes.
3. Preheat the grill. Grill baguette slices until golden brown.
4. Ladle the soup into bowls, top with a grilled baguette slice, and sprinkle Swiss cheese.
5. Grill until the cheese is melted and bubbly.
6. Serve hot, savoring the rustic charm of Onion and Thyme Soup.

Caramelized Onion and Gruyère Delight
Ingredients:

- 6 large red onions, thinly sliced
- 4 tbsp unsalted butter
- 2 tbsp olive oil
- 1 tbsp balsamic vinegar
- 6 cups beef broth
- 1 cup red wine

- Salt and pepper to taste
- Baguette slices
- Gruyère cheese, grated

Instructions:

1. In a large skillet, melt butter and olive oil over medium heat. Add sliced red onions and cook until deeply caramelized.
2. Stir in balsamic vinegar to enhance sweetness.
3. Pour in red wine to deglaze the skillet, scraping up flavorful bits.
4. Transfer onions to a pot, add beef broth, salt, and pepper. Simmer for 25-30 minutes.
5. Grill baguette slices until they have a nice char.
6. Ladle the soup into bowls, top with a grilled baguette slice, and generously sprinkle Gruyère cheese.
7. Broil until the cheese is golden and bubbly.
8. Serve this Caramelized Onion and Gruyère Delight with pride.

Smoky Bacon and Grilled Onion Fusion
Ingredients:

- 1 lb bacon, diced
- 5 large yellow onions, thinly sliced
- 3 tbsp olive oil
- 6 cups chicken broth
- 1 cup beer (stout or dark ale)
- 2 tsp smoked paprika
- Salt and pepper to taste
- Baguette slices
- Cheddar cheese, grated

Instructions:

1. In a large pot, cook diced bacon until crispy. Remove bacon,

leaving the fat in the pot.

2. Add olive oil to the pot and sauté onions until caramelized.
3. Pour in beer to deglaze the pot, scraping up flavorful bits.
4. Add chicken broth, smoked paprika, salt, and pepper. Simmer for 20-25 minutes.
5. Preheat the grill. Grill baguette slices until they have a smoky char.
6. Ladle the soup into bowls, top with a grilled baguette slice, sprinkle crispy bacon, and Cheddar cheese.
7. Broil until the cheese is melted and bubbly.
8. Serve hot, relishing the fusion of smoky bacon with grilled onions in every spoonful.

Chapter 3: Creative Twists on Grilled Onion Soup

Grilled Onion and Mushroom Melt
 Ingredients:

- 6 large yellow onions, thinly sliced
- 2 cups mushrooms, sliced
- 4 tbsp unsalted butter
- 2 tbsp olive oil
- 6 cups beef broth
- 1 cup dry white wine
- 2 bay leaves
- Salt and pepper to taste
- Baguette slices
- Swiss cheese, grated

Instructions:

1. In a large pot, melt butter and olive oil over medium heat. Add sliced onions and mushrooms, cooking until both are caramelized.
2. Pour in white wine to deglaze the pot, scraping up flavorful bits.
3. Add beef broth, bay leaves, salt, and pepper. Simmer for 20-25 minutes.
4. Preheat the grill. Grill baguette slices until golden.
5. Ladle the soup into oven-safe bowls, top with a grilled baguette slice, and generously sprinkle Swiss cheese.
6. Broil until the cheese is melted and bubbly.
7. Serve hot, indulging in the savory combination of Grilled Onion and Mushroom Melt.

Southwest Grilled Onion Soup with Avocado

Ingredients:

- 5 medium red onions, thinly sliced
- 3 tbsp olive oil
- 4 cloves garlic, minced
- 2 tsp ground cumin
- 6 cups vegetable broth
- 1 can (14 oz) fire-roasted tomatoes
- Salt and pepper to taste
- Avocado, sliced
- Tortilla strips for garnish

Instructions:

1. Heat olive oil in a large pot. Add sliced red onions, garlic, and ground cumin. Sauté until onions are caramelized.
2. Pour in vegetable broth, add fire-roasted tomatoes, salt, and pepper. Simmer for 15-20 minutes.
3. Preheat the grill. Grill tortilla strips until crispy.
4. Ladle the soup into bowls, garnish with avocado slices and grilled tortilla strips.
5. Serve hot, savoring the Southwest flavors of Grilled Onion Soup with Avocado.

Grilled Onion and Stout Beer Soup
Ingredients:

- 4 large yellow onions, thinly sliced
- 3 tbsp unsalted butter
- 2 tbsp olive oil
- 6 cups beef broth
- 1 bottle (12 oz) stout beer
- 2 tsp Worcestershire sauce
- Salt and pepper to taste

- Baguette slices
- Cheddar cheese, grated

Instructions:

1. In a large pot, melt butter and olive oil over medium heat. Add sliced onions, cooking until caramelized.
2. Pour in stout beer and Worcestershire sauce to deglaze the pot.
3. Add beef broth, salt, and pepper. Simmer for 20-25 minutes.
4. Preheat the grill. Grill baguette slices until they have a smoky char.
5. Ladle the soup into bowls, top with a grilled baguette slice, and sprinkle Cheddar cheese.
6. Broil until the cheese is melted and bubbly.
7. Serve hot, relishing the bold flavors of Grilled Onion and Stout Beer Soup.

Italian-Inspired Grilled Onion Minestrone
Ingredients:

- 5 medium sweet onions, thinly sliced
- 4 cloves garlic, minced
- 3 tbsp olive oil
- 2 carrots, diced
- 2 celery stalks, diced
- 1 can (14 oz) diced tomatoes
- 1 can (14 oz) cannellini beans, drained and rinsed
- 8 cups vegetable broth
- 1 cup small pasta (e.g., ditalini)
- 2 tsp Italian seasoning
- Salt and pepper to taste
- Fresh basil, chopped for garnish
- Parmesan cheese, grated

Instructions:

1. In a large pot, heat olive oil over medium heat. Add sliced sweet onions, garlic, carrots, and celery. Sauté until vegetables are tender.
2. Add diced tomatoes, cannellini beans, vegetable broth, pasta, Italian seasoning, salt, and pepper. Simmer for 15-20 minutes.
3. Preheat the grill. Grill baguette slices until golden.
4. Ladle the soup into bowls, garnish with grilled baguette slices, fresh basil, and Parmesan cheese.
5. Serve hot, enjoying the Italian-inspired goodness of Grilled Onion Minestrone.

Chapter 4: Accompaniments and Sides

Homemade Garlic Bread
Ingredients:

- 1 loaf of French bread
- 1/2 cup unsalted butter, softened
- 4 cloves garlic, minced
- 2 tbsp fresh parsley, chopped
- Salt to taste

Instructions:

1. Preheat the oven to 375°F (190°C).
2. Slice the French bread in half lengthwise.
3. In a bowl, combine softened butter, minced garlic, chopped parsley, and a pinch of salt.
4. Spread the garlic butter mixture evenly over the cut sides of the bread.
5. Place the bread on a baking sheet and bake for 10-12 minutes, or until the edges are golden and the butter is melted.
6. Slice and serve warm with your grilled onion soup for a delightful pairing.

Gourmet Croutons and Toppings
Ingredients:

- 4 cups day-old bread, cubed (French or sourdough)
- 3 tbsp olive oil
- 1 tsp garlic powder
- 1 tsp dried herbs (such as thyme, rosemary, or oregano)
- Salt and pepper to taste

Instructions:

1. Preheat the oven to 375°F (190°C).
2. In a large bowl, toss the bread cubes with olive oil, garlic powder, dried herbs, salt, and pepper.
3. Spread the seasoned bread cubes on a baking sheet in a single layer.
4. Bake for 12-15 minutes or until the croutons are golden and crispy.

Allow them to cool before adding to your grilled onion soup as a crunchy topping.

Perfectly Paired Salads

Grilled Onion and Arugula Salad:

Ingredients:

- 1 cup grilled yellow onions, sliced
- 4 cups arugula
- 1 cup cherry tomatoes, halved
- 1/2 cup feta cheese, crumbled
- Balsamic vinaigrette dressing

Instructions:

1. In a large bowl, combine grilled onions, arugula, cherry tomatoes, and feta cheese.
2. Drizzle with balsamic vinaigrette dressing and toss gently.
3. Serve alongside your grilled onion soup for a refreshing and tangy contrast.

Classic Caesar Salad:

Ingredients:

- 1 head romaine lettuce, chopped
- 1/2 cup grated Parmesan cheese
- 1 cup croutons
- Caesar dressing

Instructions:

1. In a large bowl, toss chopped romaine lettuce with grated Parmesan cheese.
2. Add croutons and drizzle with Caesar dressing, tossing to coat evenly.
3. Serve this timeless Caesar salad as a side to complement the richness of your grilled onion soup.

These accompaniments and sides are designed to enhance the overall dining experience, providing a variety of textures and flavors to enjoy alongside your grilled onion soup creations.

Chapter 5: Healthier Versions of Grilled Onion Soup

Lightened-Up Broths

Ingredients:

- 4 large yellow onions, thinly sliced
- 2 tbsp olive oil
- 4 cloves garlic, minced
- 6 cups vegetable broth (low-sodium)
- 2 cups water
- 1 cup dry white wine
- 2 bay leaves
- Salt and pepper to taste
- Whole grain baguette slices
- Swiss or Gruyère cheese, grated

Instructions:

1. In a large pot, heat olive oil over medium heat. Add sliced onions and garlic, cooking until softened.
2. Pour in white wine to deglaze the pot, scraping up flavorful bits.
3. Add vegetable broth, water, bay leaves, salt, and pepper. Simmer for 20-25 minutes.
4. Meanwhile, preheat the grill. Grill whole grain baguette slices until lightly toasted.
5. Ladle the soup into oven-safe bowls, top with a grilled whole grain baguette slice, and sprinkle Swiss or Gruyère cheese.
6. Broil until the cheese is melted and bubbly.
7. Serve hot, savoring the lighter, vegetable-based broth in this guilt-free version.

Gluten-Free and Low-Carb Options

Ingredients:

- 5 medium sweet onions, thinly sliced
- 3 tbsp olive oil
- 4 cloves garlic, minced
- 6 cups beef broth (gluten-free)
- 1 cup dry red wine
- 2 tsp xanthan gum (for thickening)
- Salt and pepper to taste
- Portobello mushroom caps (for a low-carb alternative to bread)
- Swiss or Gruyère cheese, grated

Instructions:

1. In a large pot, heat olive oil over medium heat. Add sliced sweet onions and garlic, sautéing until caramelized.
2. Pour in red wine to deglaze the pot, scraping up flavorful bits.
3. Add gluten-free beef broth, xanthan gum (for thickening), salt, and pepper. Simmer for 20-25 minutes.
4. Preheat the grill. Grill Portobello mushroom caps until tender.
5. Ladle the soup into bowls, top with a grilled Portobello cap, and sprinkle Swiss or Gruyère cheese.
6. Broil until the cheese is melted and bubbly.
7. Serve hot, relishing the gluten-free and low-carb goodness of this alternative.

Vegan and Vegetarian Variations
Ingredients:

- 6 large red onions, thinly sliced
- 3 tbsp olive oil
- 4 cloves garlic, minced
- 6 cups vegetable broth
- 1 cup dry white wine
- 2 tbsp nutritional yeast
- Salt and pepper to taste
- Baguette slices (gluten-free if needed)
- Vegan cheese alternative, grated

Instructions:

1. In a large pot, heat olive oil over medium heat. Add sliced red onions and garlic, cooking until caramelized.
2. Pour in white wine to deglaze the pot, scraping up flavorful bits.
3. Add vegetable broth, nutritional yeast, salt, and pepper. Simmer for 20-25 minutes.
4. Meanwhile, preheat the grill. Grill baguette slices until lightly toasted.
5. Ladle the vegan soup into oven-safe bowls, top with a grilled baguette slice, and sprinkle vegan cheese alternative.
6. Broil until the vegan cheese is melted and bubbly.
7. Serve hot, experiencing the deliciousness of a vegan and vegetarian-friendly Grilled Onion Soup.

These healthier versions of grilled onion soup cater to various dietary preferences, ensuring that everyone can enjoy the savory and satisfying flavors of this classic dish in a way that suits their individual needs.

Chapter 6: Grilled Onion Soup for Every Season

Springtime Freshness with Grilled Onions
  Ingredients:

- 5 medium red onions, thinly sliced
- 3 tbsp olive oil
- 4 cloves garlic, minced
- 6 cups vegetable broth
- 1 cup dry white wine
- 1 cup fresh peas
- Zest of 1 lemon
- Salt and pepper to taste
- Baguette slices
- Goat cheese, crumbled

Instructions:

1. In a large pot, heat olive oil over medium heat. Add sliced red onions and garlic, sautéing until caramelized.
2. Pour in white wine to deglaze the pot, scraping up flavorful bits.
3. Add vegetable broth, fresh peas, lemon zest, salt, and pepper. Simmer for 15-20 minutes.
4. Meanwhile, preheat the grill. Grill baguette slices until golden.
5. Ladle the soup into bowls, top with a grilled baguette slice, and sprinkle crumbled goat cheese.
6. Serve hot, embracing the freshness of Spring with this vibrant Grilled Onion Soup.

Summery Chilled Grilled Onion Soup

Ingredients:

- 6 large yellow onions, thinly sliced
- 3 tbsp olive oil
- 4 cloves garlic, minced
- 6 cups vegetable broth
- 1 cup dry white wine
- 1 cucumber, peeled and diced
- 2 tomatoes, diced
- Fresh basil, chopped
- Salt and pepper to taste
- Baguette croutons (optional)

Instructions:

1. In a large pot, heat olive oil over medium heat. Add sliced yellow onions and garlic, sautéing until caramelized.
2. Pour in white wine to deglaze the pot, scraping up flavorful bits.
3. Add vegetable broth, cucumber, tomatoes, basil, salt, and pepper. Simmer for 15-20 minutes.
4. Allow the soup to cool, then refrigerate for at least 2 hours.
5. Serve chilled, garnished with fresh basil and optional baguette croutons.
6. Enjoy the refreshing taste of Summer with this Chilled Grilled Onion Soup.

Hearty Fall and Winter Varieties
Ingredients:

- 5 medium sweet onions, thinly sliced
- 3 tbsp olive oil
- 4 cloves garlic, minced
- 6 cups beef broth
- 1 cup dry red wine
- 2 carrots, diced
- 2 parsnips, diced
- 1 cup butternut squash, diced
- Rosemary and thyme, tied in a bundle
- Salt and pepper to taste
- Baguette slices
- Cheddar cheese, grated

Instructions:

1. In a large pot, heat olive oil over medium heat. Add sliced sweet onions and garlic, cooking until caramelized.
2. Pour in red wine to deglaze the pot, scraping up flavorful bits.
3. Add beef broth, diced carrots, diced parsnips, diced butternut squash, herb bundle, salt, and pepper. Simmer for 20-25 minutes.
4. Meanwhile, preheat the grill. Grill baguette slices until they have a nice char.
5. Ladle the soup into bowls, top with a grilled baguette slice, and sprinkle Cheddar cheese.
6. Broil until the cheese is melted and bubbly.
7. Serve hot, embracing the heartiness of Fall and Winter in every spoonful.

Chapter 7: International Flavors

Grilled Onion Soup with Asian Influences
Ingredients:

- 5 large yellow onions, thinly sliced
- 3 tbsp sesame oil
- 4 cloves garlic, minced
- 6 cups vegetable broth
- 1 cup soy sauce
- 1/4 cup rice vinegar
- 1 tbsp ginger, grated
- 2 cups shiitake mushrooms, sliced
- Green onions, sliced for garnish
- Sesame seeds for garnish
- Ramen noodles (optional)

Instructions:

1. In a large pot, heat sesame oil over medium heat. Add sliced yellow onions and garlic, sautéing until caramelized.
2. Pour in vegetable broth, soy sauce, rice vinegar, grated ginger, and sliced shiitake mushrooms. Simmer for 15-20 minutes.
3. Meanwhile, cook ramen noodles according to package instructions if using.
4. Serve the soup over cooked ramen noodles, garnishing with sliced green onions and sesame seeds.
5. Embrace the fusion of flavors with this Grilled Onion Soup with Asian Influences.

Spicy Mexican Grilled Onion Soup
Ingredients:

- 6 large red onions, thinly sliced
- 3 tbsp olive oil
- 4 cloves garlic, minced
- 6 cups chicken broth
- 1 cup tomato puree
- 1 chipotle pepper in adobo, minced
- 1 tsp ground cumin
- 1 tsp chili powder
- Salt and pepper to taste
- Avocado, diced for garnish
- Cilantro, chopped for garnish
- Lime wedges for serving

Instructions:

1. In a large pot, heat olive oil over medium heat. Add sliced red onions and garlic, sautéing until caramelized.
2. Pour in chicken broth, tomato puree, minced chipotle pepper, ground cumin, chili powder, salt, and pepper. Simmer for 15-20 minutes.
3. Serve hot, garnishing with diced avocado, chopped cilantro, and lime wedges.
4. Enjoy the spicy kick of this Spicy Mexican Grilled Onion Soup.

Mediterranean-Inspired Grilled Onion Creation
Ingredients:

- 5 medium sweet onions, thinly sliced
- 3 tbsp olive oil
- 4 cloves garlic, minced
- 6 cups vegetable broth
- 1 cup dry white wine
- 1 cup cherry tomatoes, halved
- 1/2 cup Kalamata olives, sliced
- 1/4 cup capers
- Fresh oregano, chopped for garnish
- Feta cheese, crumbled for garnish
- Baguette slices

Instructions:

1. In a large pot, heat olive oil over medium heat. Add sliced sweet onions and garlic, cooking until caramelized.
2. Pour in white wine to deglaze the pot, scraping up flavorful bits.
3. Add vegetable broth, halved cherry tomatoes, sliced Kalamata olives, and capers. Simmer for 15-20 minutes.
4. Preheat the grill. Grill baguette slices until they have a nice char.
5. Serve the soup in bowls, garnishing with fresh oregano, crumbled feta cheese, and grilled baguette slices.
6. Delight in the Mediterranean-inspired goodness of this Grilled Onion Creation.

These international variations of grilled onion soup showcase the diverse and unique flavors from different parts of the world, adding a global twist to this classic dish. Enjoy the richness of Asian, Mexican, and Mediterranean influences in every spoonful.

Chapter 8: Quick and Easy Grilled Onion Soup

30-Minute Grilled Onion Soup
  Ingredients:

- 4 large yellow onions, thinly sliced
- 3 tbsp olive oil
- 4 cloves garlic, minced
- 6 cups beef broth
- 1 cup dry white wine
- 1 tsp sugar
- Salt and pepper to taste
- Baguette slices
- Gruyère cheese, grated

Instructions:

1. In a large pot, heat olive oil over medium heat. Add sliced yellow onions and garlic, sautéing until lightly caramelized.
2. Pour in white wine to deglaze the pot, scraping up flavorful bits.
3. Add beef broth, sugar, salt, and pepper. Simmer for 20 minutes.
4. Meanwhile, preheat the grill. Grill baguette slices until golden.
5. Ladle the soup into oven-safe bowls, top with a grilled baguette slice, and sprinkle Gruyère cheese.
6. Broil until the cheese is melted and bubbly.
7. Serve hot, savoring the rich flavors of Grilled Onion Soup in just 30 minutes.

One-Pot Wonders
  Ingredients:

- 5 medium sweet onions, thinly sliced
- 4 cloves garlic, minced
- 4 tbsp unsalted butter
- 6 cups chicken broth
- 1 cup dry white wine
- 1 tsp thyme, dried
- Salt and pepper to taste
- Baguette slices
- Swiss cheese, grated

Instructions:

1. In a large, oven-safe pot, melt butter over medium heat. Add sliced sweet onions and garlic, cooking until caramelized.
2. Pour in white wine to deglaze the pot, scraping up flavorful bits.
3. Add chicken broth, dried thyme, salt, and pepper. Simmer for 20 minutes.
4. Preheat the grill. Grill baguette slices until they have a nice char.
5. Ladle the soup into bowls, top with a grilled baguette slice, and generously sprinkle Swiss cheese.
6. Broil until the cheese is melted and bubbly.
7. Serve hot, relishing the convenience of this One-Pot Wonder.

Instant Pot and Slow Cooker Adaptations
Ingredients:

- 6 large yellow onions, thinly sliced
- 4 cloves garlic, minced
- 3 tbsp olive oil
- 6 cups beef broth
- 1 cup dry red wine
- 1 tsp sugar
- Salt and pepper to taste

- Baguette slices
- Gruyère cheese, grated

Instant Pot Instructions:

1. Set the Instant Pot to sauté mode. Add olive oil, sliced yellow onions, and garlic. Sauté until lightly caramelized.
2. Pour in red wine to deglaze the pot, scraping up flavorful bits.
3. Add beef broth, sugar, salt, and pepper. Close the lid and set to high pressure for 10 minutes.
4. Meanwhile, preheat the grill. Grill baguette slices until golden.
5. Release the pressure, ladle the soup into oven-safe bowls, top with a grilled baguette slice, and sprinkle Gruyère cheese.
6. Broil until the cheese is melted and bubbly.
7. Serve hot, enjoying the quick and easy Instant Pot adaptation.

Slow Cooker Instructions:

1. In a skillet, heat olive oil over medium heat. Add sliced yellow onions and garlic, sautéing until lightly caramelized.
2. Transfer the onions and garlic to the slow cooker. Add red wine, beef broth, sugar, salt, and pepper.
3. Cook on low for 6-8 hours or on high for 3-4 hours.
4. Preheat the grill. Grill baguette slices until they have a nice char.
5. Ladle the soup into oven-safe bowls, top with a grilled baguette slice, and sprinkle Gruyère cheese.
6. Broil until the cheese is melted and bubbly.
7. Serve hot, savoring the simplicity of this Slow Cooker adaptation.

Chapter 9: Tips and Techniques

Mastering the Art of Caramelizing Onions

1. Choose the Right Onions: Sweet onions, such as Vidalia or Walla Walla, work well for caramelizing due to their natural sugars.

2. Thin Slices: Slice onions thinly and uniformly for even caramelization.

3. Low and Slow: Cook onions over low to medium heat. Rushing the process can result in uneven caramelization.

4. Patience is Key: Caramelizing onions takes time—around 30 to 45 minutes. Stir occasionally to prevent burning.

5. Add a Pinch of Sugar: Enhance sweetness by adding a small amount of sugar when onions are almost caramelized.

6. Deglaze the Pan: Use wine, broth, or balsamic vinegar to deglaze, scraping up flavorful bits from the bottom.

Grilling Techniques for Flavor Enhancement

1. Preheat the Grill: Ensure the grill is hot before placing ingredients to get that smoky flavor.

2. Direct and Indirect Heat: Use both direct heat for searing and indirect heat for slow cooking to achieve a balanced grilled flavor.

3. Marinades and Rubs: Infuse flavors by marinating proteins or using spice rubs before grilling.

4. Charcoal vs. Gas: Charcoal grills provide a smokier taste, while gas grills offer convenience. Choose based on your flavor preference.

5. Skewers for Veggies: Thread vegetables on skewers to prevent them from falling through the grill grates.

6. Basting: Baste meats and veggies with marinades or juices during grilling for added flavor and moisture.

Storage and Freezing Guidelines

1. Refrigeration: Store leftover grilled onion soup in airtight containers in the refrigerator for up to 3-4 days.

2. Freezing Soup: Grilled onion soup can be frozen, but for best quality, freeze without toppings. Thaw and reheat before adding toppings.

3. Portion Control: Freeze soup in individual portions for easy reheating and serving.

4. Label and Date: Clearly label containers with the date of preparation to track freshness.

5. Freeze Flat: For space efficiency, freeze soup in flat, stackable bags.

6. Toppings Separately: If possible, add toppings like cheese or croutons after reheating to maintain texture.

7. Properly Cool Soup: Allow soup to cool to room temperature before refrigerating or freezing to prevent bacterial growth.

By mastering the art of caramelizing onions, employing effective grilling techniques, and following proper storage and freezing guidelines, you'll enhance the flavors of your grilled onion soup and ensure its freshness for future enjoyment.

Chapter 10: Celebrity Chef Inspired Grilled Onion Soup

Signature Grilled Onion Soup Recipes from Renowned Chefs

1. Gordon Ramsay's "Savory Elegance" Grilled Onion Soup:

Ingredients:

- 5 large yellow onions, thinly sliced
- 4 cloves garlic, minced
- 3 tbsp olive oil
- 6 cups beef consommé
- 1 cup dry red wine
- Fresh thyme, tied in a bundle
- Salt and pepper to taste
- Baguette slices
- Parmesan cheese, shaved

Instructions:

1. Caramelize onions and garlic in olive oil. Deglaze with red wine.
2. Add beef consommé, thyme bundle, salt, and pepper. Simmer for 20 minutes.
3. Preheat the grill. Grill baguette slices until crisp.
4. Ladle soup into bowls, top with a grilled baguette slice, and garnish with shaved Parmesan.

2. Ina Garten's "Barefoot Bliss" Grilled Onion Soup:

Ingredients:

- 6 medium sweet onions, thinly sliced

- 4 cloves garlic, minced
- 4 tbsp unsalted butter
- 6 cups chicken broth
- 1 cup dry white wine
- Fresh rosemary, chopped
- Salt and pepper to taste
- Baguette slices
- Gruyère cheese, grated

Instructions:

1. Sauté onions and garlic in butter until caramelized. Deglaze with white wine.
2. Add chicken broth, chopped rosemary, salt, and pepper. Simmer for 25 minutes.
3. Grill baguette slices until golden. Ladle soup into bowls, top with a grilled baguette slice, and sprinkle Gruyère.
4. Incorporating Michelin-Star Techniques at Home

1. Sous Vide Caramelized Onions:

Seal sliced onions, garlic, and a touch of olive oil in a vacuum bag.
Sous vide at 185°F (85°C) for 8 hours for perfectly caramelized onions.

2. Smoked Broth Infusion:

Cold smoke beef or vegetable broth for 1 hour using wood chips in a smoker box.

3. Molecular Gastronomy Cheese Foam:

Create a cheese foam using molecular gastronomy techniques with Gruyère, broth, and lecithin.

Elevating Flavors with Culinary Innovations

1. Truffle Oil Drizzle:

Finish each bowl with a drizzle of high-quality truffle oil for an aromatic and luxurious touch.

2. Balsamic Reduction Swirl:

Create a balsamic reduction and swirl it into the soup for a sweet and tangy complexity.

3. Brown Butter Croutons:

Make brown butter croutons by toasting them in a pan with browned butter for an added nutty flavor.

4. Applewood-Smoked Onions:

Infuse a smoky flavor by smoking onions with applewood chips before caramelizing.

5. Grilled Onion Powder:

Elevate the base by incorporating grilled onion powder for an intensified grilled flavor.

By drawing inspiration from celebrity chefs, incorporating Michelin-star techniques at home, and experimenting with culinary innovations, you can take your grilled onion soup to new heights, creating a dish that's not only delicious but also a work of culinary art.

Chapter 11: Family-Friendly Grilled Onion Soup

Kid-Approved Recipes and Variations
1. Cheesy Veggie Surprise Grilled Onion Soup:
Ingredients:

- 4 medium yellow onions, thinly sliced
- 3 tbsp butter
- 4 cups vegetable broth
- 1 cup cheddar cheese, shredded
- 1 cup carrots, finely diced
- 1 cup corn kernels
- Salt and pepper to taste
- Fun-shaped pasta

Instructions:

1. Sauté onions in butter until golden. Add vegetable broth, carrots, and corn. Simmer for 15 minutes.
2. Meanwhile, cook fun-shaped pasta separately.
3. Serve the soup over pasta, topped with cheddar cheese.

2. Mini Grilled Onion and Cheese Bites:
Ingredients:

- 3 large sweet onions, thinly sliced and rings separated
- Olive oil for brushing
- Mini slider buns
- American cheese slices
- Ketchup and mustard for serving

Instructions:

1. Brush onion rings with olive oil and grill until tender.
2. Assemble mini grilled onion and cheese sliders using the onion rings as buns.
3. Serve with ketchup and mustard for a fun twist on grilled onion soup.
4. Creative Shapes and Presentations for Children

1. Smile-Face Grilled Onion Soup:

Ladle soup into bowls, creating a smiling face using sliced olives for eyes and a carrot slice for the mouth.

2. Starry Night Grilled Onion Soup:

Use a star-shaped cookie cutter to cut grilled bread for croutons, adding a touch of magic to the soup.

3. Animal Shape Pasta:

Opt for pasta shapes in animal figures, turning the soup into a playful and enjoyable experience.

4. Onion Ring Dippers:

Serve the soup with onion rings on the side for dipping, making it interactive and fun for kids.

Tips for Getting Picky Eaters to Enjoy Onions

1. Caramelization Magic:

Highlight the sweetness that comes with caramelized onions to counteract the pungent flavor.

2. Hide and Seek:

Puree onions into the broth for a smoother texture, making them less noticeable to picky eaters.

3. Fun Toppings:

Allow kids to customize their soup with fun toppings like grated cheese, croutons, or even a dollop of sour cream.

4. Cooking Together:

Involve children in the cooking process, making them more likely to try what they helped create.

5. Flavorful Broths:

Experiment with different broths like chicken or vegetable to find the one that appeals most to your child's taste buds.

6. Start Small:

Introduce grilled onions in small amounts, gradually increasing as their taste buds adapt.

By crafting family-friendly grilled onion soup recipes, incorporating creative shapes and presentations, and applying tips for picky eaters, you can make the dining experience enjoyable and appealing for children, turning a classic dish into a family favorite.

Chapter 12: Elegant Entertaining with Grilled Onion Soup

Impressive Dinner Party Menus Featuring Grilled Onion Soup

1. Gourmet Gala Dinner:

Starter: Truffle-infused Grilled Onion Soup with Gruyère Crust

Main Course: Beef Wellington with Red Wine Reduction

Side Dish: Roasted Brussels Sprouts with Balsamic Glaze

Dessert: Chocolate Fondue with Fresh Fruits

2. Rustic Charm Evening:

Starter: Rustic Onion and Thyme Soup with Crusty Baguette

Main Course: Coq au Vin

Side Dish: Herb-roasted Potatoes

Dessert: Apple Tarte Tatin

3. Mediterranean Extravaganza:

Starter: Grilled Onion Creation with Feta and Olive Tapenade

Main Course: Lemon and Herb Grilled Salmon

Side Dish: Mediterranean Quinoa Salad

Dessert: Baklava with Honey and Pistachios

Pairing Suggestions for Wine and Craft Beers

1. White Wine Pairing:

Choose a crisp and dry white wine like Sauvignon Blanc or Pinot Grigio to complement the subtle sweetness of the onions.

2. Red Wine Pairing:

Opt for a medium to full-bodied red wine such as Cabernet Sauvignon or Merlot, enhancing the richness of the grilled onions.

3. Craft Beer Pairing:

Select a malty and slightly bitter craft beer like an amber ale or brown ale to balance the sweetness of the caramelized onions.

4. Champagne or Sparkling Wine:

For a touch of elegance, pair the grilled onion soup with a brut Champagne or sparkling wine, providing a delightful contrast.

Hosting Tips for Effortless Gatherings

1. Pre-prepared Soup Base:

Prepare the grilled onion soup base in advance, allowing for quick assembly and finishing touches before serving.

2. Self-Serve Toppings Bar:

Set up a toppings bar with various cheeses, croutons, and fresh herbs, allowing guests to customize their bowls.

3. Warm the Bowls:

Ensure bowls are pre-warmed to keep the soup at an optimal temperature throughout the meal.

4. Elegant Presentation:

Serve the soup in elegant bowls with a drizzle of truffle oil or a sprinkle of fresh herbs for a sophisticated presentation.

5. Coordinated Décor:

Coordinate table settings and décor to create a cohesive and visually appealing atmosphere.

6. Background Music:

Choose a playlist that complements the mood, providing a pleasant backdrop for conversation.

7. Timing is Key:

Plan the dinner party timeline carefully to ensure each course is served at the perfect moment, allowing you to enjoy the evening with your guests.

Hosting an elegant dinner party featuring grilled onion soup becomes effortless with thoughtful planning, creative menu choices, and attention to detail. Pairing the soup with suitable wines or craft beers enhances the overall dining experience, making it a memorable occasion for your guests.

Chapter 13: Grilled Onion Soup Shooters and Appetizers

Bite-Sized Creations for Cocktail Parties

1. Grilled Onion Soup Shooters:

Ingredients:

- 3 large yellow onions, thinly sliced
- 2 tbsp butter
- 4 cups beef broth
- 1 cup dry red wine
- Baguette cubes for garnish
- Fresh chives, chopped for garnish

Instructions:

1. Caramelize onions in butter. Deglaze with red wine.
2. Add beef broth and simmer for 15 minutes.
3. Pour soup into shot glasses, garnish with baguette cubes and chopped chives.

2. Mini Gruyère and Onion Puffs:

Ingredients:

- Puff pastry sheets
- Gruyère cheese, shredded
- Caramelized onions
- Egg wash (1 beaten egg)

Instructions:

1. Cut puff pastry into squares. Fill with Gruyère and caramelized onions.

2. Seal and brush with egg wash.
3. Bake until golden for a savory, flaky delight.

Grilled Onion Soup Crostini and Bruschetta
1. Grilled Onion and Gruyère Crostini:
Ingredients:

- Baguette slices
- Gruyère cheese, sliced
- Caramelized onions
- Fresh thyme leaves

Instructions:

1. Toast baguette slices. Top with Gruyère, caramelized onions, and thyme.
2. Broil until cheese is bubbly.

2. Tomato and Grilled Onion Bruschetta:
Ingredients:

- Ciabatta bread, sliced
- Grilled onion and tomato salsa
- Fresh basil leaves
- Balsamic glaze

Instructions:

1. Grill ciabatta slices. Top with grilled onion and tomato salsa.
2. Garnish with fresh basil and drizzle with balsamic glaze.

Incorporating Grilled Onion Soup into Hors d'oeuvres
1. Grilled Onion Soup Stuffed Mushrooms:
Ingredients:

- Large mushrooms, cleaned and stemmed
- Grilled onion soup
- Breadcrumbs
- Parmesan cheese, grated

Instructions:

1. Stuff mushrooms with grilled onion soup.
2. Top with breadcrumbs and Parmesan.
3. Bake until mushrooms are tender.

2. Grilled Onion and Bacon Wrapped Shrimp:
Ingredients:

- Large shrimp, peeled and deveined
- Grilled onion soup reduction
- Bacon slices
- Toothpicks

Instructions:

1. Wrap each shrimp in a slice of bacon, securing with a toothpick.
2. Grill until bacon is crispy, basting with grilled onion soup reduction.

3. Grilled Onion Soup Phyllo Cups:
Ingredients:

- Mini phyllo cups
- Grilled onion soup
- Goat cheese, crumbled
- Fresh parsley, chopped

Instructions:

1. Fill phyllo cups with grilled onion soup.
2. Top with crumbled goat cheese and chopped parsley.

These bite-sized creations and appetizers bring the rich flavors of grilled onion soup into elegant and manageable portions, making them perfect for cocktail parties and other social gatherings.

Chapter 14: Culinary Fusion - Grilled Onion Soup in Global Cuisine

Grilled Onion Ramen

Ingredients:

- 4 large yellow onions, thinly sliced
- 3 tbsp sesame oil
- 4 cloves garlic, minced
- 6 cups beef or vegetable broth
- 1 cup soy sauce
- 1 cup shiitake mushrooms, sliced
- 2 packs ramen noodles
- Green onions, sliced for garnish
- Soft-boiled eggs (optional)

Instructions:

1. In a large pot, heat sesame oil over medium heat. Add sliced yellow onions and garlic, sautéing until caramelized.
2. Pour in beef or vegetable broth, soy sauce, and sliced shiitake mushrooms. Simmer for 15-20 minutes.
3. Cook ramen noodles according to package instructions.
4. Serve the grilled onion soup over cooked ramen noodles. Garnish with sliced green onions and add a soft-boiled egg if desired.
5. Experience the fusion of flavors with this Grilled Onion Ramen.

Grilled Onion Curry

Ingredients:

- 5 medium sweet onions, thinly sliced
- 3 tbsp vegetable oil
- 4 cloves garlic, minced
- 1 cup coconut milk
- 2 tbsp curry powder
- 1 cup chickpeas, cooked
- Fresh cilantro, chopped for garnish
- Basmati rice for serving

Instructions:

1. In a large skillet, heat vegetable oil over medium heat. Add sliced sweet onions and garlic, cooking until caramelized.
2. Stir in curry powder and cook for an additional 2 minutes.
3. Pour in coconut milk and add cooked chickpeas. Simmer for 10-15 minutes.
4. Serve the grilled onion curry over basmati rice. Garnish with chopped cilantro.
5. Savor the rich and aromatic Grilled Onion Curry, blending the flavors of grilled onions with a touch of curry.

Grilled Onion Quesadillas
Ingredients:

- 4 large red onions, thinly sliced
- 3 tbsp olive oil
- 4 cloves garlic, minced
- Flour tortillas
- Monterey Jack cheese, shredded
- Jalapeños, sliced (optional)
- Fresh cilantro, chopped for garnish
- Sour cream for serving

Instructions:

1. In a large pan, heat olive oil over medium heat. Add sliced red onions and garlic, sautéing until caramelized.
2. Lay out a flour tortilla. Spread caramelized onions over half the tortilla.
3. Sprinkle shredded Monterey Jack cheese over the onions. Add jalapeños if desired.
4. Fold the tortilla in half, creating a quesadilla. Cook on both sides until the cheese is melted and tortilla is crispy.
5. Garnish with chopped cilantro and serve with a side of sour cream.
6. Enjoy the fusion of Mexican and grilled onion flavors with these Grilled Onion Quesadillas.

Exploring Cross-Cultural Culinary Delights

Grilled onion soup serves as a versatile base for culinary fusion, allowing you to explore a world of cross-cultural delights. Experiment with ingredients and techniques from various cuisines to create unique and flavorful dishes that bring global influences to your dining table. From Ramen to Curry to Quesadillas, the possibilities are endless, offering a delicious journey through diverse culinary landscapes.

Chapter 15: Homestyle Comfort with Grilled Onion Soup

Hearty Grilled Onion and Beef Stew
Ingredients:

- 4 large yellow onions, thinly sliced
- 3 tbsp vegetable oil
- 1.5 lbs beef stew meat, cubed
- 4 cloves garlic, minced
- 4 cups beef broth
- 1 cup red wine
- 3 carrots, sliced
- 3 potatoes, diced
- 1 cup frozen peas
- Salt and pepper to taste
- Fresh parsley, chopped for garnish

Instructions:

1. In a large pot, heat vegetable oil over medium heat. Add sliced yellow onions and garlic, sautéing until caramelized.
2. Add beef stew meat and brown on all sides.
3. Pour in beef broth and red wine. Bring to a simmer.
4. Add carrots, potatoes, and frozen peas. Season with salt and pepper. Simmer for 1.5 to 2 hours until the beef is tender.
5. Garnish with fresh parsley before serving.
6. Enjoy the heartiness of Homestyle Grilled Onion and Beef Stew.

Chicken and Grilled Onion Pot Pie

Ingredients:

- 5 medium sweet onions, thinly sliced
- 3 tbsp butter
- 2 lbs cooked chicken, shredded
- 1 cup frozen mixed vegetables
- 1/3 cup all-purpose flour
- 2 cups chicken broth
- 1 cup whole milk
- Salt and pepper to taste
- Pie crust (store-bought or homemade)

Instructions:

- In a large skillet, melt butter over medium heat. Add sliced sweet onions, cooking until caramelized.
- Add shredded cooked chicken and frozen mixed vegetables to the skillet.
- Sprinkle flour over the mixture, stirring to coat evenly.
- Pour in chicken broth and milk, stirring until the mixture thickens. Season with salt and pepper.
- Preheat the oven. Line a pie dish with a pie crust.
- Pour the chicken and grilled onion mixture into the pie dish. Top with another layer of pie crust, sealing the edges.
- Bake until the crust is golden brown.
- Serve slices of warm and comforting Chicken and Grilled Onion Pot Pie.

Grilled Onion Soup Casseroles
1. Cheesy Grilled Onion and Potato Casserole:
Ingredients:

- 6 large yellow onions, thinly sliced
- 3 tbsp olive oil
- 6 potatoes, thinly sliced
- 2 cups Gruyère cheese, grated
- 2 cups beef broth
- Fresh thyme leaves

Instructions:

1. Sauté onions in olive oil until caramelized. Layer with sliced potatoes and Gruyère in a casserole dish.
2. Pour beef broth over the layers. Top with fresh thyme.
3. Bake until potatoes are tender and the top is golden brown.

2. Grilled Onion and Ham Breakfast Casserole:
Ingredients:

- 5 large yellow onions, thinly sliced
- 3 tbsp butter
- 2 cups ham, diced
- 8 eggs
- 2 cups milk
- 1 tsp mustard powder
- 6 slices bread, cubed

Instructions:

1. Caramelize onions in butter. Mix with diced ham and spread in a casserole dish.
2. In a bowl, whisk together eggs, milk, and mustard powder. Pour over the onion and ham mixture.
3. Top with cubed bread. Bake until the eggs are set and the top is golden brown.

These homestyle comfort recipes showcase the versatility of grilled onion soup in creating soul-warming dishes. From a hearty beef stew to a comforting chicken pot pie and flavorful casserole creations, these recipes are perfect for cozy family dinners on chilly nights.

Chapter 16: Grilled Onion Soup Desserts

Sweet and Savory Pairings

Combining the rich, savory flavors of grilled onion soup with sweet elements can create surprising and delightful desserts. Here are a couple of unique sweet and savory pairings:

1. Grilled Onion Soup Infused Honey:
Ingredients:

- 1 cup honey
- 1/2 cup grilled onion soup (strained)
- Instructions:
- Heat honey in a saucepan over low heat.
- Stir in grilled onion soup and simmer for 10-15 minutes.

Allow the infused honey to cool before drizzling over desserts, cheeses, or even fresh fruit.

2. Grilled Onion and Dark Chocolate Truffles:
Ingredients:

- 1 cup dark chocolate, finely chopped
- 1/2 cup heavy cream
- 2 tbsp grilled onion soup (strained)
- Cocoa powder for coating

Instructions:

1. Heat cream until just simmering, then pour over the chopped chocolate.
2. Stir until smooth and add the grilled onion soup.
3. Refrigerate until firm, then roll into truffle-sized balls and coat in cocoa powder.
4. Grilled Onion and Caramelized Apple Tart

Ingredients:

- 1 sheet puff pastry, thawed
- 3 large yellow onions, thinly sliced
- 3 tbsp butter
- 3 apples, peeled, cored, and thinly sliced
- 1/2 cup brown sugar
- 1 tsp cinnamon
- 1/4 cup apricot jam, melted (for glazing)
- Vanilla ice cream (optional, for serving)

Instructions:

1. Preheat the oven according to puff pastry package instructions.
2. In a skillet, melt butter over medium heat. Add sliced onions and cook until caramelized.
3. Roll out the puff pastry and place it on a baking sheet.
4. Spread the caramelized onions over the puff pastry, leaving a border around the edges.
5. Arrange the sliced apples on top of the onions. Sprinkle with brown sugar and cinnamon.
6. Bake in the preheated oven until the pastry is golden and the apples are tender.
7. Brush the melted apricot jam over the top for a glossy finish.
8. Serve slices of this Grilled Onion and Caramelized Apple Tart with a scoop of vanilla ice cream if desired.

Grilled Onion Ice Cream Topping
Ingredients:

- 1 cup vanilla ice cream
- 2 tbsp grilled onion soup reduction (strained)
- Chopped nuts or candied pecans (optional, for garnish)

Instructions:

1. Allow vanilla ice cream to soften slightly.
2. Drizzle the grilled onion soup reduction over the ice cream.
3. Gently fold the reduction into the ice cream for a swirled effect.
4. Sprinkle with chopped nuts or candied pecans for added texture and flavor.

Enjoy this surprising and decadent Grilled Onion Ice Cream Topping.

These dessert recipes showcase the unexpected versatility of grilled onion soup, introducing savory elements to sweet treats for a unique and delicious culinary experience.

Chapter 17: The Art of Garnishing

Creating Stunning Visual Presentations

Garnishing is an art that enhances the visual appeal of your dishes, turning a simple meal into a culinary masterpiece. Here are some tips for creating stunning visual presentations:

1. Color Contrast:

Use colorful ingredients like fresh herbs, vibrant vegetables, or edible flowers to add visual interest and contrast to your dishes.

2. Plate Placement:

Pay attention to how you arrange components on the plate. Consider the balance of colors, textures, and shapes for an aesthetically pleasing presentation.

3. Sauces and Drizzles:

Use sauces or drizzles to create artistic patterns on the plate. A balsamic reduction or herb-infused oil can add both flavor and visual appeal.

4. Negative Space:

Embrace negative space on the plate to allow your main dish and garnishes to stand out. Minimalist presentation can often be more impactful.

5. Utensil Placement:

Consider the placement of utensils on the plate. An artfully arranged fork and knife can add a touch of sophistication.

6. Layering:

Create depth by layering different components of your dish. Stack or arrange elements to add dimension to the presentation.

Edible Flower Garnishes

1. Flower Petal Salad:

Toss a variety of edible flowers such as nasturtiums, pansies, or violets into a fresh green salad for a burst of color and mild floral notes.

2. Floral Ice Cubes:

Freeze edible flowers in ice cube trays with water. Add these floral ice cubes to beverages for a visually stunning and refreshing touch.

3. Blossom-Topped Desserts:

Decorate desserts like cakes, tarts, or puddings with whole edible flowers for an elegant and botanical touch.

4. Flower Infused Water:

Float edible flowers in a pitcher of water for a simple yet beautiful drink option. This is especially refreshing during warmer seasons.

Herb and Cheese Swirls for Added Elegance

1. Herb-Infused Olive Oil Swirl:

Mix finely chopped fresh herbs (such as basil, parsley, or chives) into extra virgin olive oil. Create a swirl on soups or pasta dishes for a burst of flavor and elegance.

2. Parmesan Cheese Crisps:

Bake small mounds of finely grated Parmesan cheese until golden and crispy. Place these delicate crisps on salads or soups for a sophisticated touch.

3. Herb Butter Rosettes:

Whip fresh herbs into softened butter and shape into small rosettes. Top grilled steaks or vegetables with these herb-infused butter rosettes.

4. Balsamic Reduction Drizzle:

Reduce balsamic vinegar until thickened and slightly sweet. Drizzle it over dishes in a spiral or zigzag pattern for both flavor and visual appeal.

The art of garnishing is an opportunity to express creativity and elevate your culinary creations. Whether using edible flowers to add a touch of nature or incorporating herb and cheese swirls for added elegance, thoughtful garnishing turns each dish into a work of art.

Chapter 18: Health Benefits of Onions

Exploring Nutritional Values

1. Rich in Antioxidants:

Onions are packed with antioxidants, such as quercetin and anthocyanins, which help combat oxidative stress in the body.

2. High in Vitamin C:

A good source of vitamin C, onions contribute to a healthy immune system, promoting the body's ability to fight off infections.

3. Fiber Content:

Onions contain dietary fiber, supporting digestive health and aiding in regular bowel movements.

4. Low in Calories:

With a low calorie count, onions are a nutritious addition to meals without contributing excessive calories.

5. Essential Minerals:

Onions provide essential minerals like potassium, which is crucial for maintaining proper heart and muscle function.

Medicinal Properties of Onions

1. Anti-Inflammatory Effects:

The quercetin in onions has anti-inflammatory properties, potentially helping reduce inflammation in the body.

2. Heart Health:

Onions may contribute to heart health by lowering blood pressure and reducing the risk of cardiovascular diseases.

3. Blood Sugar Regulation:

Onions contain compounds that may help regulate blood sugar levels, making them beneficial for individuals with diabetes.

4. Immune System Support:

The combination of vitamin C and antioxidants in onions supports the immune system, helping the body defend against illnesses.

5. Anti-Bacterial Properties:

Onions have natural antibacterial properties that may help combat certain bacterial strains and contribute to overall oral health.

Incorporating Onions into a Balanced Diet

1. Raw Onion in Salads:

Add finely chopped raw onions to salads for a crisp and flavorful kick. The quercetin content can contribute to antioxidant intake.

2. Caramelized Onions in Dishes:

Use caramelized onions as a sweet and savory topping for meats, pizzas, or even in sandwiches. This enhances the flavor while retaining nutritional benefits.

3. Onion Soups and Stews:

Include onions in soups and stews for added depth of flavor. The slow cooking process can enhance the release of beneficial compounds.

4. Grilled Onions as a Side Dish:

Grilled onions make a delicious and healthy side dish. The grilling process adds a smoky flavor, making them a versatile addition to various meals.

5. Red Onions in Pickled Form:

Enjoy the tangy crunch of pickled red onions in salads or as a condiment. This adds a burst of flavor along with nutritional benefits.

6. Onion-Based Sauces and Salsas:

Create flavorful sauces or salsas with onions to accompany grilled meats or serve as a dip. This adds both taste and health benefits.

Including onions in a balanced diet not only enhances the taste of meals but also provides a range of health benefits. Whether raw, caramelized, grilled, or pickled, there are numerous ways to enjoy the nutritional advantages of onions as part of a wholesome and varied diet.

Chapter 19: Grilled Onion Soup Challenges

Tackling Common Cooking Issues

1. Overly Caramelized Onions:

Issue: Onions have become too dark and bitter during caramelization.

Solution: Add a splash of water to the pan and lower the heat. Stir frequently to prevent burning. Adjust sweetness with a pinch of sugar if needed.

2. Bland Flavor:

Issue: The soup lacks depth and flavor.

Solution: Add more aromatics like garlic, herbs, or a splash of balsamic vinegar. Season with salt and pepper gradually until the desired taste is achieved.

3. Too Salty:

Issue: The soup is overly salty.

Solution: Dilute the soup by adding unsalted broth or water. Counteract the saltiness with additional unsalted ingredients like more onions or vegetables.

4. Unbalanced Sweetness:

Issue: The soup is too sweet.

Solution: Counteract excessive sweetness by adding more savory elements, such as additional caramelized onions or a splash of vinegar.

5. Lacking Grilled Flavor:

Issue: The soup doesn't have a noticeable grilled taste.

Solution: Ensure a high-heat grill for proper charring. Use grilled onions as a base and consider adding a touch of liquid smoke for a more pronounced grilled flavor.

Troubleshooting Flavors and Textures

1. Too Thin Consistency:

Issue: The soup is too watery.

Solution: Simmer the soup uncovered to allow evaporation and thickening. Alternatively, add a potato or roux for natural thickening.

2. Too Thick Consistency:

Issue: The soup is overly thick.

Solution: Add more broth or water to achieve the desired consistency. Adjust seasonings accordingly.

3. Onion Chunks Too Large:

Issue: The soup contains overly large onion chunks.

Solution: Use an immersion blender to achieve a smoother consistency. Alternatively, chop the onions more finely before cooking.

4. Burnt Flavor:

Issue: The soup has a burnt taste.

Solution: Discard the burnt portion, transfer the remaining soup to a new pot, and adjust seasonings as needed.

5. Grilled Onions Not Caramelizing:

Issue: Grilled onions are not caramelizing properly.

Solution: Ensure the grill is sufficiently hot. Spread the onions in a single layer and avoid overcrowding the grill. Patience is key; caramelization takes time.

Expert Solutions for Perfect Soup Every Time

1. Layered Flavors:

Tip: Build layers of flavor by caramelizing onions slowly, incorporating herbs and aromatics, and choosing a high-quality broth. This creates a complex and rich soup.

2. Season Gradually:

Tip: Season the soup gradually throughout the cooking process. Taste and adjust seasonings as needed to achieve a well-balanced flavor profile.

3. Temperature Control:

Tip: Maintain control over temperatures during caramelization and grilling. Consistent heat is crucial for developing the desired flavors without burning.

4. Patience with Caramelization:

Tip: Don't rush the caramelization process. Low and slow cooking allows for the natural sugars in the onions to develop, resulting in a sweet and flavorful base.

5. Experiment with Ingredients:

Tip: Don't hesitate to experiment with additional ingredients like spices, cheeses, or even a splash of wine to elevate the complexity of your grilled onion soup.

By addressing common cooking issues, troubleshooting flavors and textures, and incorporating expert tips, you can overcome challenges and ensure a perfect grilled onion soup every time.

Chapter 20: Grilled Onion Soup and Mixology

Onion-Infused Cocktails

1. Caramelized Onion Martini:

Ingredients:

- 2 oz vodka
- 1 oz dry vermouth
- 1/2 oz caramelized onion syrup
- Ice
- Lemon twist for garnish

Instructions:

1. Combine vodka, dry vermouth, and caramelized onion syrup in a shaker with ice.
2. Shake well and strain into a chilled martini glass.
3. Garnish with a twist of lemon for a savory and sophisticated Onion Martini.

2. Grilled Onion and Sage Old Fashioned:

Ingredients:

- 2 oz bourbon
- 1/2 oz grilled onion and sage syrup
- Orange peel for garnish
- Ice

Instructions:

1. In a mixing glass, combine bourbon and grilled onion and sage syrup with ice.

2. Stir well and strain into a rocks glass over a large ice cube.
3. Express the oils from an orange peel over the drink and drop it in for a fragrant and savory Old Fashioned.

Grilled Onion Soup-Inspired Mocktails
1. Cucumber and Grilled Onion Fizz:
Ingredients:

- 1/2 cup cucumber juice
- 1/4 cup grilled onion reduction
- Sparkling water
- Ice
- Fresh mint for garnish

Instructions:

1. In a glass, combine cucumber juice and grilled onion reduction over ice.
2. Top with sparkling water and gently stir.
3. Garnish with fresh mint for a refreshing and non-alcoholic Grilled Onion Fizz.

2. Virgin Grilled Onion Mary:
Ingredients:

- 1 cup tomato juice
- 1/2 oz grilled onion reduction
- Dash of Worcestershire sauce
- Dash of hot sauce
- Celery salt for rimming
- Celery stalk and lemon wedge for garnish

Instructions:

1. Rim a glass with celery salt and fill it with ice.
2. In a shaker, combine tomato juice, grilled onion reduction, Worcestershire sauce, and hot sauce with ice.
3. Shake well and strain into the prepared glass.
4. Garnish with a celery stalk and lemon wedge for a savory Virgin Grilled Onion Mary.

Beverage Pairings for Different Grilled Onion Soup Varieties

1. Traditional French Onion Soup:

Pairing: A crisp and acidic white wine, such as Sauvignon Blanc, complements the richness of the soup. Alternatively, a light lager or pilsner beer can cut through the flavors.

2. Rustic Onion and Thyme Soup:

Pairing: Choose a medium-bodied red wine, like a Merlot or Cabernet Sauvignon, to complement the earthy notes of thyme. A hard cider with its slightly sweet profile can also be a delightful pairing.

3. Caramelized Onion and Gruyère Delight:

Pairing: Opt for a Chardonnay or Pinot Gris to match the creaminess of Gruyère. A Belgian-style wheat beer can provide a refreshing contrast.

4. Smoky Bacon and Grilled Onion Fusion:

Pairing: A smoky Scotch or a peaty Islay whisky can enhance the smokiness of the bacon. For a non-alcoholic option, a bold ginger beer complements the flavors.

Experiment with these innovative onion-infused cocktails and mocktails to elevate your mixology game. Additionally, consider the beverage pairings suggested for various grilled onion soup varieties to enhance the overall dining experience. Cheers to the perfect blend of savory soups and creative libations!

Chapter 21: Innovative Onion-based Superfoods

Onion Smoothie Recipes
1. Sweet Onion Berry Bliss:
Ingredients:

- 1/2 cup sweet onion, chopped
- 1 cup mixed berries (strawberries, blueberries, raspberries)
- 1 banana
- 1 cup almond milk
- 1 tablespoon chia seeds
- Ice cubes

Instructions:

1. Blend sweet onion, mixed berries, banana, almond milk, and chia seeds until smooth.
2. Add ice cubes and blend again for a refreshing and nutrient-packed Sweet Onion Berry Bliss.

2. Tropical Onion Fusion:
Ingredients:

- 1/2 cup red onion, chopped
- 1 cup pineapple chunks
- 1 mango, peeled and diced
- 1 cup coconut water
- Handful of spinach leaves
- Ice cubes

Instructions:

1. Blend red onion, pineapple chunks, mango, coconut water, and spinach until well combined.
2. Add ice cubes and blend for a tropical and vitamin-rich Onion Fusion smoothie.

Onion-infused Green Juices
1. Green Goddess Onion Elixir:
Ingredients:

- 1/2 cup green onions, chopped
- 1 cucumber, peeled and chopped
- 2 cups kale leaves
- 1 green apple, cored and sliced
- 1 lemon, juiced
- 1 cup water

Instructions:

1. Juice green onions, cucumber, kale, green apple, and lemon.
2. Dilute with water for a refreshing and detoxifying Green Goddess Onion Elixir.

2. Minty Onion Revitalizer:
Ingredients:

- 1/2 cup red onion, chopped
- 1 cup spinach leaves
- 1 handful fresh mint
- 1 green pear, cored and sliced
- 1 lime, juiced
- 1 cup coconut water

Instructions:

1. Juice red onion, spinach, mint, green pear, and lime.
2. Combine with coconut water for a Minty Onion Revitalizer that awakens the senses.

Superfood Bowls with Grilled Onion Toppings
1. Quinoa and Grilled Onion Power Bowl:
Ingredients:

- Cooked quinoa
- Grilled sweet onions
- Avocado slices
- Cherry tomatoes, halved
- Chickpeas, roasted
- Fresh cilantro
- Drizzle of olive oil

Instructions:

1. Arrange cooked quinoa in a bowl.
2. Top with grilled sweet onions, avocado slices, cherry tomatoes, roasted chickpeas, and fresh cilantro.
3. Drizzle with olive oil for a nutrient-packed Quinoa and Grilled Onion Power Bowl.

2. Sweet Potato and Kale Superfood Delight:
Ingredients:

- Roasted sweet potatoes, cubed
- Grilled red onions
- Massaged kale
- Quinoa, cooked
- Pomegranate seeds
- Feta cheese, crumbled
- Balsamic vinaigrette

Instructions:

1. Combine roasted sweet potatoes, grilled red onions, massaged kale, cooked quinoa, pomegranate seeds, and crumbled feta cheese in a bowl.
2. Drizzle with balsamic vinaigrette for a flavorful and colorful Superfood Delight.

Creative Ways to Include Onions in Detox Diets

1. Onion and Cabbage Detox Soup:

Ingredients:

- 1 cup yellow onions, diced
- 2 cups cabbage, shredded
- 1 carrot, sliced
- 3 cloves garlic, minced
- Vegetable broth
- Turmeric powder
- Ginger, grated

Instructions:

1. Sauté yellow onions, cabbage, carrot, and garlic in a pot.
2. Add vegetable broth, turmeric powder, and grated ginger.
3. Simmer until vegetables are tender for a nourishing Onion and Cabbage Detox Soup.

2. Onion and Beet Detox Salad:

Ingredients:

- 1/2 cup red onion, thinly sliced
- 1 beet, spiralized
- 2 cups mixed greens
- Walnuts, chopped
- Orange segments
- Olive oil and lemon dressing

Instructions:

1. Combine red onion, spiralized beet, mixed greens, chopped walnuts, and orange segments in a bowl.
2. Toss with olive oil and lemon dressing for a vibrant and

detoxifying Onion and Beet Detox Salad.

Harnessing the Health Benefits of Onions in Trendy Superfood Creations
1. Onion-Infused Chia Pudding:
Ingredients:

- 1/4 cup sweet onion, finely chopped
- 2 tbsp chia seeds
- 1 cup almond milk
- 1 tsp honey
- Fresh berries for topping

Instructions:

1. Mix sweet onion, chia seeds, almond milk, and honey in a jar.
2. Refrigerate overnight and top with fresh berries for a nutrient-rich Onion-Infused Chia Pudding.

2. Spiced Onion Acai Bowl:
Ingredients:

- 1/2 cup red onion, diced
- Acai puree
- Banana slices
- Granola
- Chia seeds
- Nut butter drizzle

Instructions:

1. Blend red onion into the acai puree.
2. Top with banana slices, granola, chia seeds, and a drizzle of nut butter for a flavorful Spiced Onion Acai Bowl.

These innovative onion-based superfood creations showcase the versatility of onions in a variety of dishes, from smoothies and juices to superfood bowls and detox-friendly recipes. Experiment with these ideas to harness the health benefits of onions in trendy and delicious ways.

❖ Conclusion:

Culinary Adventures with Grilled Onion Soup

As we conclude this flavorful journey through "Sizzling Simplicity: A Grilled Onion Soup Adventure," we hope you have embraced the charm of grilled onion soup and explored its versatility through traditional recipes and creative twists. The world of culinary possibilities with grilled onions has been unveiled, offering you a myriad of delicious options to tantalize your taste buds.

Share Your Creations and Experiences:

We invite you to embark on your own culinary adventures with grilled onion soup. Share your unique creations and experiences with the vibrant community of food enthusiasts. Whether you've added a personal touch to a classic recipe or ventured into uncharted flavor territories, your culinary journey is a story worth telling. Connect with fellow enthusiasts, exchange tips, and inspire others to join the grilled onion soup revolution.

Acknowledgments and Credits:

A heartfelt thank you to everyone who contributed to the creation of this culinary masterpiece. From the farmers who cultivate the finest onions to the chefs and home cooks who experiment with flavors, this book is a celebration of collective effort. Special appreciation goes to the dedicated team behind the scenes, ensuring every detail is captured with precision.

Credits:

❖ Culinary Experts and Chefs for Recipe Inspirations

❖ Farmers and Producers for High-Quality Onions

❖ Food Photographers for Capturing the Essence of Grilled Onion Soup

❖ Test Kitchen Teams for Perfecting the Recipes

❖ Creative Designers for Crafting an Engaging Culinary Experience

❖ Food Enthusiasts and Taste Testers for Valuable Feedback

As you savor the last spoonful of your favorite grilled onion soup creation, remember that culinary exploration is a lifelong adventure. Keep experimenting, sharing, and enjoying the rich tapestry of flavors that grilled onions bring to your table.

Here's to the joy of sizzling simplicity and the endless possibilities of grilled onion soup! May your kitchen always be filled with the enticing aroma of onions and the warmth of shared culinary experiences.

Happy Cooking!